# Out
## of the Cauldron

# Out
# of the Cauldron

A SHORT HISTORY OF WITCHCRAFT

by Bernice Kohn

HOLT, RINEHART AND WINSTON

New York · Chicago · San Francisco

*Unless otherwise indicated, the pictures in this book
were obtained through the facilities of the
New York Public Library Picture Collection.
The illustrations for Chapter 9 are from the
Rare Book Division of the New York Public Library.*

FOR DAVID
WHO BEWITCHED ME FROM THE START

# Contents

# 1

# Which Is a Witch?

A cavern. In the middle, a boiling cauldron. Thunder. Enter the three Witches.

FIRST WITCH: Thrice the brinded cat hath mew'd.

SECOND WITCH: Thrice and once the hedge-pig whined.

THIRD WITCH: Harpier cries, 'Tis time, 'tis time.

FIRST WITCH: Round about the cauldron go;
In the poison'd entrails throw.
Toad, that under cold stone
Days and nights has thirty-one
Swelter'd venom sleeping got,
Boil thou first i' the charmed pot.

ALL:                    Double, double, toil and trouble;
                        Fire burn and cauldron bubble.

SECOND WITCH:   Fillet of a fenny snake,
                        In the cauldron boil and bake;
                        Eye of newt and toe of frog,
                        Wool of bat and tongue of dog,
                        Adder's fork and blind-worm's
                        sting,
                        Lizard's leg and owlet's wing,
                        For a charm of powerful trouble,
                        Like a hell-broth boil and bub-
                        ble.

ALL:                    Double, double toil and trouble;
                        Fire burn and cauldron bubble.

THIRD WITCH:    Scale of dragon, tooth of wolf,
                        Witches' mummy, maw and gulf
                        Of the ravin'd salt-sea shark,
                        Root of hemlock digg'd i' the
                        dark,
                        Liver of blaspheming Jew
                        Gall of goat, and slips of yew
                        Sliver'd in the moon's eclipse,
                        Nose of Turk and Tartar's lips,
                        Finger of birth-strangled babe
                        Ditch-deliver'd by a drab,
                        Make the gruel thick and slab:
                        Add thereto a tiger's chaudron,
                        For the ingredients of our caul-
                        dron.

| | |
|---|---|
| ALL: | Double, double toil and trouble: |
| | Fire burn and cauldron bubble. |
| SECOND WITCH: | Cool it with a baboon's blood, |
| | Then the charm is firm and good. |

This is how William Shakespeare, in the play *Macbeth,* describes three witches making a "witches' brew." The description fits the ideas that most people have about witches' potions. As for the ladies themselves, they are always pictured as hideous hags, quite as ugly as their nasty recipe.

Throughout the Middle Ages when the persecution of witches was a popular sport in Europe, the image was similar. The witch was generally thought to be an old hag. She was said to fly through the night on a broomstick or on the back of an animal to attend a meeting with the Devil. She had what was called a "familiar," an animal that was really a demon in disguise. Since almost no one kept house pets in those days, the mere possession of a cat, a dog, a bird—or even a toad in the garden—was often enough to brand one a witch.

Supposedly, the hag had made a pact with the Devil and was his dutiful slave. The Devil always left a mark upon her body, and this mark was taken as another proof of witchhood. Many a poor old woman was burned at the stake because she had the misfortune to have a birthmark on her shoulder.

Possession of small dolls, or lumps of wax or clay resembling human figures was also proof of guilt. It was a popularly accepted notion that witches could cause pain, injury, or death by sticking pins or nails into images of their victims.

Almost everyone believed that witches had strange and fearsome powers. It was said that they could cause milk to sour, hens to stop laying; that they could bring thunder and lightning, hail and drought. Even educated people were certain that witches could make babies sicken and die, prevent women from becoming pregnant or make them have miscarriages, dry up a mother's milk, cause plagues of locusts, set fires, kill cattle, sheep, or crops, and call forth any sort of disease or misfortune. No wonder witches were feared!

It was also common belief that good witches could break the spells of evil witches. Good witches could effect magical cures, give charms and amulets for protection, compound powerful medicines of herbs, and concoct "guaranteed" love potions.

It was thought that witches performed ceremonies that mocked Christian rituals. They were supposed to renounce Christianity, spit upon the cross, say the Lord's Prayer backwards, and use

Two witches brewing a charm.

sacramental wafers stamped with the Devil's name.
It was also claimed that witches had sexual orgies
with the Devil and murdered infants in order to
eat their flesh.

What are the facts about witches? Did they ever really exist? Do they exist now? If they do, what are they like? Are they always old and ugly? Are they born or made? Are witches the same as magicians or sorcerers? Are they always evil?

Throughout the centuries, different segments of society have had different answers to those questions. Although witchcraft (or the belief in it) has been a powerful force in the world since before recorded history, it has always been the subject of a great deal of confusion. It still is. Unfortunately, much of our information about witchcraft has come from its detractors. Much of it has come from accused witches who made elaborate confessions under torture. As a result, most of what has passed for factual information has been strongly biased and often patently untrue.

Witches have long been feared, and countless numbers of people have been convicted—or merely accused—of practicing witchcraft and have been put to death. On the other hand, in many societies, witches have been (and are today) among the most highly respected members of the community.

Undoubtedly, our knowledge of witchcraft is compounded of both fact and fiction. While we may never succeed in separating the two, let's examine the data in some detail and see what we can make of them.

# 2

# The Beginnings of Witchcraft

The origins of witchcraft, like many of its rituals, are hidden in mystery. Out of the welter of theories that have been advanced, one particularly "educated guess" stands out: It is that true witchcraft was a very old religion.

While most authorities are in agreement on this point today, it wasn't until 1921 that the idea was convincingly presented for the first time. It was then that Professor Margaret Alice Murray, a well-known anthropologist, wrote a book called *The Witch-Cult in Western Europe*. The book provided a basis, or at least a taking-off point, for every serious student of European witchcraft who followed.

Dr. Murray claims that witchcraft is the remnant of a pagan religion that dates from paleolithic (early Stone Age) times. The sexual rites and orgies, which have become so large a part of witchcraft's lore, were the ancient fertility rituals performed by primitive peoples everywhere to insure the continuance of life through birth.

Other scholars, following Dr. Murray's lead, have taken us even further along. They have pointed out that certain ceremonial aspects of Christianity, Judaism, and other relatively modern religions, all sprang from the same old pagan roots and so it is not surprising that some common elements remain.

During the Middle Ages, the Christian Church became the great enemy of witchcraft contending that witches worshiped the Devil and perverted certain Christian practices. It is possible that what seemed like a mockery of Christian ritual may have been an earlier form of the same ritual. It is also true, of course, that after the growth of Christianity, bits and pieces of Christian ceremonies found their way into witch rites. Even today, this mixture is found wherever witchcraft and another religion are practiced at the same time by large portions of the population. Africa, Haiti, and Polynesia are examples. The ancient rites may be

**A.** A Witch.
**B.** A Spirit raised by the Witch.
**C.** A Friar raising his Imps.
**D.** A Fairy Ring.
**E.** A Witch rideing on the Devill through the Aire.
**F.** An Inchanted Castle.

Elements of witchcraft, Christianity, fairy magic, and enchantment can all be found in this curious nineteenth-century chart entitled "Sorceries."

heavily influenced by the common religion of the land.

The Old Religion theory gives us one explanation for another mystery. In every part of the world where witchcraft exists, there are certain common beliefs and practices. Even today, a witch doctor in a remote jungle, cut off completely from the rest of the world, may stick a pin through a doll to kill an enemy; a witch deep in the German forest did exactly the same thing hundreds of years ago. It would seem that as Stone Age man spread over the face of the globe, he took his magical religion with him.

On the other hand, there are some students who believe that even without any common heritage, primitive man, in scattered locations, would have arrived at the same superstitions, beliefs, and rituals anyway. All early people were concerned with birth, death, growth, light, darkness, and other natural phenomena. Rituals built around these major influences introduced fertility, blood, plants, the sun and moon into all religions. The hazards, difficulties, problems, and calamities of life seemed less frightening with the belief that they could be influenced by ritual of some sort.

In any case, it is quite clear that early witchcraft *was* a religion. And as Christianity became more firmly established in Europe, witchcraft was more and more feared and hated. It was totally confused with sorcery and magic, as well as every kind of evil practice.

By the ninth century, a Church decree declared that signing pacts with the Devil and flying through the air were impossibilities. The decree instructed priests to preach against these false ideas and to teach instead that such myths arose because the Evil Spirit may have sent phantasms or dreams of flying. The decree became part of canon law, and it was strictly forbidden to believe in flying or in meetings with the Devil. Law or not, many believed.

One of the Church's problems in eradicating beliefs in witchcraft and other forms of supernatural phenomena was that such beliefs were deeply ingrained in the entire population. Even the priests themselves could not easily give up the teachings of their homes and families, and almost all theologians were convinced that evil spirits abounded and that witches were able to employ their services. If it was usual for priests to hold on to some of the pre-Christian beliefs, it was universal for the uneducated masses. The Church decree was a lost cause in the face of so much resistance.

As time passed, anti-witch feeling began to increase, and we begin to feel the full flavor of it in a definition of a witch written in 1594 by William West, an English lawyer. He said:


A Witch or hag is she which being eluded by a league made with the Devil through his persuasion, inspiration and juggling, thinketh she can design what manner of things soever, either by thought or imprecation, as to shake the air with lightnings and thunder, to cause hail and tempests, to remove green corn or trees to another place, to be carried of her familiar which hath taken upon him the deceitful shape of a goat, swine, calf, etc., into some mountain far distant, in a wonderful short space of time. And sometimes to fly upon a staff or fork, or some other instrument. And to spend all the night after with her sweetheart, in playing, sporting, banqueting, dalliance, and diverse other devilish lusts, and lewd desports, and to show a thousand such monstrous mockeries.

The old ideas were so slow to die that three hundred years after West's writings, there were others that were clearly reminiscent of them. Typical was a book called *Aradia, or the Gospel of the Witches.* It was written by another Englishman, Charles Leland in 1899 and was based on a collection of folklore. The book contained a witch's gospel that

Leland claimed had been given to him by an Italian witch. The gospel is a potpourri of other religions, ancient and modern. One passage reads:

You shall make cakes of meal, wine, salt and honey in the shape of the crescent moon, and say: "I do not bake the bread, nor with it salt, nor do I cook the honey with the wine: I bake the body and the blood and the soul, the soul of Diana, that she know neither rest nor peace, and ever be in cruel suffering till she will grant what I request, what I do most desire, I beg it of her from my very heart! and if the grace be granted, O Diana! in honor of thee will I hold this feast and drain the goblet deep, we will dance and wildly leap, and if thou grantest the grace which I require, then when the dance is wildest, all the lamps shall be extinguished and we will freely love!" And thus shall it be done: all shall sit down to supper all naked, men and women, and the feast over, they shall dance and sing and make music, and then love in the darkness, with all lights extinguished; for it is the spirit of Diana who extinguishes them, and so will they dance and make music in her praise.

The impact of this pagan outpouring on late-nineteenth-century England can only be imagined! There must have been many people in whom it struck a familiar chord, for The Old Religion had never died out completely in Europe. It was always carried on, sometimes deliberately, sometimes quite innocently.

Before medical science developed, witches were the only doctors. Everyone who was ill consulted the local witch for a magical spell or more to the point, a herbal medicine. Witches were, in fact, well versed in the use of herbs, and quite likely

Consultation with a witch.

the remedies they concocted were often very effective.

People also consulted witches when they wanted to harm others. The witch's special occult or psychic powers were considered to be inborn, but the knowledge and lore of magic was handed down from generation to generation.

Often, these practices continued long after witchcraft as such had been almost forgotten. For example, the fairies, or little folk of Ireland, are thought by some modern scholars to have been witches. Surely every Irish child heard stories of the fairies and their magical powers. And just as surely, good Christian Irish mothers had no idea that they were teaching anything that had to do with witchcraft.

During the fifteenth and sixteenth centuries, when witch hunts were rampant, many an odd old woman, despised by the other villagers, chose to become a witch. She may have done so for social reasons since she was an outcast elsewhere; or, fed up with her neighbors' contempt, she may have hoped to come by the power to do them harm.

The greatest number of these "first generation" witches were probably never witches at all. Thousands of them were burned, hanged, or otherwise killed in Europe, and a few lost their lives in

America. They usually had been tried and found guilty. Some confessed freely. Many confessed under torture. Some never confessed but were found guilty anyway. The witch trials made a farce of justice and were a blot upon the history of the human race.

# 3

# The Witch Trials

Even though laws against witches had been on the books for a long time, they were not enforced in deadly earnest until the late 1400's. What happened then seems unbelievable. It was almost as if the whole world went mad at once.

A partial explanation of the hysteria may have been the plague of the Black Death that had recently swept through Europe leaving misery and despair in its wake. Between 1347 and 1350 it claimed nearly one-fourth of the entire population. Among a superstitious people, it is almost automatic to blame misfortunes on supernatural forces rather than natural ones. Many deaths were blamed on witches.

Even though the Black Death had long since come and gone, the interest in witches remained intense. People saw witches wherever they looked. No one was safe from suspicion. A next-door neighbor, a friend, a relative, anyone at all might be taken for a witch. If the cream failed to make butter in the churn, if a cow died, a barn burned, or a crop was poor, it was believed that a witch had used the evil eye or cast a spell. Every witch had to be rooted out.

At the same time, there were strong stirrings of dissatisfaction in the Christian Church. This was the movement that would soon lead to the Protestant Reformation in the early part of the sixteenth century, and it was causing a great deal of anxiety. Under the threat of a split in the Church, anything that even hinted of heresy was suspect.

It must be understood that the charge of heresy could not be made against anyone who was not a baptized member of the Church. A heretic was a Christian who either preached doctrines or followed practices that were against those of the Church. Such persons were considered to be outstandingly dangerous because of the possibility of their leading others into error. Heretics ran the double risk (as have non-conformists in every age) of being viewed simultaneously as confused and disorganized yet easily capable of commiting such complex crimes as treason, anarchy, or murder.

Now, in the late 1400's, although the Church had earlier ridiculed the popular notion of witchcraft and had flatly stated that people could fly only in dreams, it suddenly seemed clear that there were witches and that witches were heretics—and with this discovery, reason was abandoned.

Much was made of the so-called Black Mass that witches were supposed to celebrate. There is strong doubt that the Black Mass was ever a part of true witchcraft practice. While there was probably some admixture of witchcraft and Christianity, the Black Mass itself was very possibly the invention of those eager to prove how heretical witches were.

There are several versions of what the Black Mass consists of. Some claim that it is a Catholic Mass recited backwards. Others maintain that the proper Mass is used as a framework but embroidered with heresies. For example, the celebrant of the Black Mass is said to be a mock priest clothed in black but without a cross. He stands with his back to the altar and instead of the Host he elevates a piece of black turnip. At that signal all of the witches call out to the Devil, "Master, help us!"

There are some recorded versions of the ritual that are much more grisly. In one, a naked woman lies upon the altar with a chalice on her stomach. An infant is slaughtered, and its blood is caught in the chalice.

Almost all accounts of the Black Mass involve a sacrifice. Usually, however, it is not a child that is said to be killed, but an animal, and preferably a black one.

Dr. Murray tells us that in many ancient cults, the god (a human leader) reigned for only one year and was sacrificed at the end of this time. Later, a goat was used for sacrifice instead.

In any case, it was undoubtedly this accusation of heretical acts by witches plus the threat of Protestantism that led to a reversal of Church opinion. Now everyone spoke openly about witches' flights to midnight meetings and the murders of unbaptized babies for sacrificial purposes. The general excitement spurred the Church to act, and in 1484 Pope Innocent VIII issued a bull, a papal letter, which ordered an inquisition to wipe out witches. The bull stated in part:

It has indeed lately come to our ears, not without afflicting us with bitter sorrow, that. . .many persons of both sexes, unmindful of their own salvation and straying from the Catholic Faith, have abandoned themselves to devils, incubi and succubi, and by their incantations, spells, conjurations, and other accursed charms and crafts, enormities and horrid offences, have slain infants yet in the mother's womb. . .and at the instigation of the Enemy of Mankind they do not shrink from committing and perpetrating the foulest abominations and filthiest excesses to the deadly peril of their own souls. . .

The papal bull was amazingly successful. The witch hunts raged across Europe for two centuries. After the Reformation of the sixteenth century, the hunts were taken up by the Protestants and even made their way to the New World. Some historians have stated that 300,000 witches were put to death in Europe. One writer claims that about 100,000 were burned in Germany alone during the seventeenth century. The figures for executions in Britain range all the way from 1000 to 70,000.

Starting out, perhaps, with motives that were purely religious, the witch hunts soon became a form of political juggling and, often, open and

This sixteenth-century German woodcut shows the burning of three witches.

outrageous fortune hunting. It was extremely easy to remove a political rival and claim his worldly goods simply by accusing him of practicing witchcraft or of harboring a wife who did so. It was surely more than coincidence that when the wealthy were executed, their property was often divided up among their accusers. Any kind of testimony was accepted in court. Witnesses were often young children or known criminals.

Although the courts of the time were generally not noted for justice, the witch trials did not even make a pretense of being fair or impartial. It was understood that witches had extraordinary powers and had to be gotten out of the way before they had a chance to do mischief.

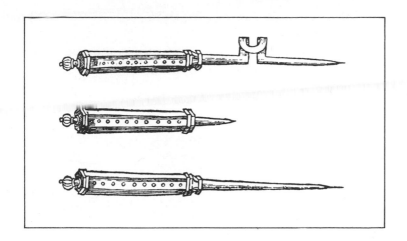

Three prickers' pins used to test supposed Devil's Marks.   STUDIO BRIGGS.

The accused were stripped naked, completely shaved and searched (often in public) for Devil's Marks. An old scar, a mole, a mark of any kind was proof that the Devil had left his sign.

Since Devil's Marks were not supposed to bleed, men known as witch-prickers became busy professionals during the witch hunts. When a mark was found, the pricker skillfully inserted a pin into it and almost always proved that his victim was indeed a witch. Though in some cases, there is no clear explanation for this, it is fairly easy to understand how an experienced pricker could insert the point of a pin just under the surface of a corn, a callous, or an old scar without drawing blood.

Another "absolute proof" of witchcraft was the discovery of a Witch's Mark, an "extra teat" on any woman. Again, a wart, a protruding mole, a small bump on any part of the body at all was assumed to be a teat from which the woman fed milk to her animal familiar.

Lacking marks, it was considered desirable to obtain a confession. This could almost always be done by means of torture. Prisoners were hung by the hands from a rope, flogged, burned on the soles of the feet. They also had fingers smashed with thumbscrews, legs smashed in a machine called the boot, and bodies stretched on the ladder or rack. When the accused could stand no more, if he didn't die, he generally confessed.

Every now and then there were a few prisoners who kept absolutely silent and died of torture. It is likely that these were not recent converts to witchcraft but were, in an unbroken family line, real practitioners of The Old Religion handing down their secrets—and keeping them in the family—from dim paleolithic days. Their own faith and belief gave them strength to face death silently as countless religious martyrs of all persuasions have done.

On the other hand, there were many persons who confessed freely to witchcraft without any torture

The torture chamber of the Inquisition.

at all. Some of these people actually believed that
they were guilty of all sorts of crimes and were
eager to talk about them. We see their counterparts now. Whenever news of an unsolved murder

is printed in the newspapers, the police expect to hear from a few false "murderers." Today, these people are known to be ill and if found to be severely ill are sent to mental hospitals. Then, they were all executed. No one would have dreamed of questioning the validity of a confession. The common way to kill a witch was to burn one alive.

England never reached quite the same pitch of witch hysteria as the rest of Europe. Torture was not legally permitted—although there are many occasions of it in English history. In general, however, the accused witches were given more civilized trials and some were even found innocent and released. Those who were not, were hanged rather than burned.

# 4

## The Coven and the Sabbat

The details of witches' organization and rites are, by now, a mixture of fact and fancy. What follows here is the lore as it exists. You may draw your own conclusions as to its truth.

Although some experts disagree, it is generally accepted that the basic unit of witch organization was the coven. A coven consisted of thirteen persons—a Grand Master and twelve witch members.

It is interesting to note the importance of the group of thirteen throughout history. Jesus had twelve disciples. King Arthur had twelve knights. Robin Hood had twelve men—and they all wore green, the fairy color. A modern jury consists of twelve jurors presided over by a judge. In England, the Order of the Garter was founded with two groups of thirteen. And so on.

A curious observation has been made about the last example, the Order of the Garter. This is the highest order of British knighthood and it was founded by Edward III in about 1348. The garter seems a strange item on which to found any such organization—but the garter was an extremely important article of dress to members of the witch cult. It was considered a badge of membership. To this day, British folk dancers wear a garter when they do the Morris dance. They say they wear it because it is "traditional," but no one knows how the tradition started. It is probable that the Order of the Garter came into being partly (if not entirely) because of that same forgotten tradition. There *is* a story about a Countess's garter falling off during a ball and the king pinning it to his own leg to spare the lady embarrassment. The story may or may not be true, but it is doubtful that such a trivial incident would result in anything as important and lasting as the Order.

Dr. Murray has a much more interesting hypothesis. She points out that the king, as chief of the Order, wore a mantle covered with 168 garters. On his leg, he wore one more making a total of

169—or thirteen times thirteen—a highly magical number. (Even today, there are many superstitions connected with the number thirteen. For example, many modern buildings have no thirteenth floor, and many people consider the thirteenth of the month an unlucky day.) Taking into account the garters, the magic numbers, and coven-sized groups, Dr. Murray suggests the possibility that those first two groups of the Order were really two covens!

The word "coven" itself comes from the Latin *convenire,* to come together. The words "convent" and "convene" come from the same root.

A coven is thought to have met about once a week (or whenever convenient for its members), and the meeting was called an *esbat.* The esbat was always held at night, and, while the dates of the gatherings may have been somewhat irregular, there was always an esbat on the night of the full moon. There may have been some primitive, ritual-istic moon worship involved and on a practical level, for people traveling on foot through the forest, it was certainly an advantage to travel by full moonlight rather than in the dark. There are no accurate records of what happened at an esbat. Possibly it was more or less a "business" meeting, with discussion of past deeds and future plans. And just before the meeting ended at dawn, there was probably some dancing.

But several times a year, all of the covens within traveling distance gathered together for a large, gala meeting. This was called a *sabbat*. The word "sabbat" is frequently confused with Sabbath, but most experts agree that there is no connection be-

The celebration of a witches' sabbat, as drawn from a sixteenth-century French engraving.    THE GRANGER COLLECTION.

tween the two. Dr. Murray believes that sabbat comes from a French word that means "to frolic."

The sabbats were indeed frolics. They were large, gay, boisterous assemblies, and dancing was a prominent feature. It is easy to understand that the newly formed Protestants were even more outraged by witches than the Catholics had been. The "loose," flamboyant, and joyous carousing was contrary to every Puritanical belief.

The sabbat was held at an ancient religious site, often near a lake or a stream in the heart of a forest. Other popular sites were a crossroads where several forest paths met, a cave, a secluded spot near fairy mounds or heaps of earth of stones. (Joan of Arc was suspected of witchcraft when she was seen dancing around a "fairy tree" at Domrémy.)

Unlike the esbat, the sabbat was always held on certain definite dates. The origins of these dates are lost in antiquity, but it is interesting that the folklore surrounding the sabbats were powerful enough to have perpetuated most of them as holidays right up until the present time.

The spring and fall sabbats were the most important ones. The first festival of the year was on the eve of May Day, or April 30th. It was called Roodmas in England and Walpurgis Nacht (night) in Germany. May Day is still a traditional day for May Pole (fairy tree) dancing.

The fall sabbat came on October 31st, All Hallow Eve, the time of an ancient Druidic festival. We, of course, celebrate Hallowe'en on this date and feature a motif of witches.

The less important dates for sabbats were Candlemas, February 2nd; Lammas, August 1st; St. Thomas Day, December 21st, and the Eve of St. John, June 23rd. All of these sabbat dates were established long before the same dates became Christian holidays.

Legend tells us that on the night of a sabbat, there was only one way for a witch to get to the gathering. She removed her clothing, rubbed her body with oil or ointment, and flew on her broomstick. She left the house through the chimney or a window.

Recipes for "flying oil" vary, and a number of them have been handed down to us through word of mouth or old books or records. There is, of course, no way to judge whether or not the recipes were actually prepared this way. One of the most popular formulas has as its main ingredients the fat of a young baby, several kinds of herbs, and soot!

Whether the recipes are accurate or not, there

is good reason to believe that witches did actually rub themselves with oil. Many primitive peoples today use ointments on their bodies before they dance, and athletes often do the same before a sporting event. Incidentally, we might wonder where the custom of crowning kings with holy oil originated.

Witches' oil, like athletes' oil, may have been used just as a lubricant and muscle rub before the lengthy and energetic dancing that would take place at the sabbat. But more probably, in addition to the innocent-sounding herbs of the old recipes, the oil contained powerful drugs that were absorbed into the blood stream and caused hallucinations. Scientists have attested to the fact that there *are* drugs that can produce this effect, especially if applied to mucous membrane areas of the body. This may be one of the reasons for the many confessions of flying. Even without drugs, flying dreams are very common. An impressionable person might easily think that the dreams were real.

As for leaving the house by a means other than the door, the explanation offered was a simple one. Witches were thought to avoid doors because most houses were protected by iron or salt. It was believed that witches could not be close to either of those substances, so homeowners nailed horseshoes

The Devil appears to his followers.

above the door and sprinkled salt on the doorstep. They also sprinkled salt around the baby's crib.

So leaving by window or chimney, the witch took off for the secret meeting place. The chief of the sabbat was thought to be the Devil himself or his representative. He was called variously, the Grand Master, Satan, the Priest, Lucifer, Beelzebub, and so on.

The Devil always appeared with a tail, fiery eyes, and horns. Sometimes he wore a hood on his head, sometimes he was completely covered by an animal skin. He was always masked. The mask was made in such a way as to give the man inside it a deep and hollow voice.

Other features of the costume were cloven shoes, claws, ass's ears, terrible teeth, and a sulphurous smell. The Devil usually wore black and often had a tall hat and a garter. Sometimes the witches knew who their Master was in private life, often they did not and really believed that he was a supernatural being. U. S. 1636504

The procedure at the sabbat differed slightly in its details from place to place. One of the common practices was the so-called Kiss of Shame, kissing the Devil below his tail to pay him homage. There may have been a more elaborate meeting than that at the esbat with reports from witches from all parts of the district on spells, successes, and failures. There was usually a roll call to check attendance.

With all of that out of the way, it was time for the great and most important feature of the sabbat, the dancing. This was done to music, and it is said that all of the dancers were naked. They burned sulphur and incense and carried flaming torches. It is quite likely that hallucinogenic drugs were used freely. The dancing was wild and totally abandoned. Finally, following the custom of ancient fertility rites, the dance turned into an orgy.

Sometime before daybreak, a feast was served. Whether it was ordinary food or a cannibal banquet of human meat as was often charged is unknown.

The sabbat ended just before the first light. The witches must have made quite a picture, drunk on wine, excitement, and drugs, utterly exhausted by the night of revelry, picking their way through the forest to enter their homes before the other villagers awoke.

As the weary witches reach their beds, it is interesting for us to examine some counterparts of these witch procedures in much, much earlier times.

Margaret Murray traces the witch cult back to a pre-Christian era when the goddess Diana was worshiped throughout western Europe. Diana was the moon goodess as well as the goddess of fertility. Dr. Murray points out that the dates of the chief sabbats, May Eve and November Eve, show that they go back to a time that was still pre-agricultural. Since they did not refer to planting or harvesting, it appears that the rites performed were chiefly for the purpose of promoting fertility in animals. It is a well-established fact that primitive peoples believe strongly in sympathetic magic: when the dance culminated in sexual intercourse, it would promote fertility among women; when the participants wore the guise of animals, the fertility of animals would be encouraged. By the same reasoning, partaking of a feast would make food plentiful.

Who the forerunner of the Devil was in ancient times, even Dr. Murray does not guess. If we consult Sir James Frazer's *The Golden Bough,* we learn only that Diana was assisted by her priest, the god of the grove. Frazer tells us that Virbius was the lover or consort of Diana—but that little is known of him save his name. Not much help!

We do learn however, that the Druids, pre-Christian Celtic priests who inhabited Gaul, Britain, and Ireland, met in sacred forest groves. Their festivals fell at about the same times as the sabbats: they lit fires, danced, and feasted. They also sacrificed humans to increase the fertility of the land.

Julius Caesar, in *De Bello Gallico,* tells us this about the Druids:

The whole Gaulish nation is to a great degree devoted to superstitious rites; and on this account those who are afflicted with severe diseases, or who are engaged in battles and dangers, either sacrifice human beings for victims, or vow that they will immolate themselves; these employ the Druids as ministers for such sacrifices, because they think that, unless the life of man be repaid for the life of man, the will of the immortal gods cannot be appeased.

We also know of the Druids that they were deeply religious; there was a Head or Chief of some sort who presided over their rites; they counted time by nights and figured a year on revolutions of the moon.

The point of this excursion into past history is simply this: there was a flourishing pagan religion throughout Europe before Christ. No religion that has existed for hundreds or thousands of years has ever been wiped out by decree. It is almost impossible to believe that underneath the veneer of Christianity, there was not still a remnant of The Old Religion during the Middle Ages.

Who were the medieval witches, anyway? With few exceptions, they were women. We do not know why this was so, but in many cultures it is more common for women rather than men to be involved in religious rites and observances.

Most of the witches (although not all) were peasants or members of the lower classes. (Again, it is common for the less educated to cling to old ways and superstitions.) Some had been dedicated

A Druid sacrifice, as pictured by a nineteenth-century
artist.

to the cult by their mothers when they were born. The others were converts. Of these, some were converted by witch friends. Some were disturbed persons or misfits who seized the opportunity to behave at the sabbat in a way that would have been totally socially unacceptable anywhere else. Many were stupid, handicapped, or downtrodden women who could not gain status in any other way. And some had consulted witches in the past for help in getting rid of an enemy or for aid of some sort. Since clients of witches were punished by the Church if found out, some of these people considered it safer to drop away from the Church altogether and join with the witches instead.

According to the information we have, when a witch was converted into the cult she went through three major steps. These were the giving of formal consent, denial of Catholic faith, and making a pact with the Devil.

The lore tells us that when the would-be witch was presented to the coven, she defied her Christian faith by spitting on the cross or insulting the Virgin Mary. She then placed one hand on her head, the other on the sole of her foot and pledged to the Devil all that was in between. A "baptismal" rite followed, and the novice was given a new name.

Now she made her pact with the Devil. Sometimes it was a spoken oath, sometimes a written contract. If the latter, it was signed in blood. The signature was probably a mark since few women knew how to write. The pact was not usually for life but for a definite period of years, most often seven (another ancient magical number). During this time, the witch pledged complete obedience to the Devil. In return, she was guaranteed his protection with that of all the other witches. In addition, she would learn the secrets that would give her special powers.

The initiation ended with a sacrifice (often a black hen), the enrolling of the new name in the Black Book (the coven's rollbook), and the giving of the Devil's Mark. The mark was made by tatooing, by forcing colored mud under the skin to form a raised area, by a bite, a claw scratch, or a paw print of a hare, a bat, or some other animal.

Devil's Marks were made anywhere on the body but common spots were the shoulders, the finger, or a hidden spot such as the genitals, the armpit, or the underside of the eyelid. The marking, perhaps the entire ceremony, took place while the novice was under the influence of drugs. When the rites ended, she was a full-fledged witch.

Although witches' rites must have varied from

place to place, the accounts that have come down to us are remarkably similar. This may be ascribed at least in part to the fact that at the trials, the inquisitors asked such leading questions as to almost "put the words into the mouth" of the accused. Under extreme torture, there was undoubtedly eagerness to please the questioner by giving the "right" answers.

# 5

## Some Famous Witches

The so-called witches whose stories we know today are the ones whose trials became a matter of history. Perhaps the most famous of them all was Joan of Arc. During most of the period of witch hunts—from the fourteenth through the seventeenth centuries—witches were pursued by both Church and state. The Church made its accusations on the grounds of heresy. The state prosecutions were often political. Joan of Arc was attacked by both factions.

By the beginning of the fifteenth century, heresy or religious dissent of any kind was often a mask for national ambition or rivalry. Several crusades to stamp out heresy had resulted in the political subjugation of one people by another.

When the Hundred Years' War began in 1336, it was largely a feudal conflict without religious implications. In time, it became a highly nationalistic struggle between France and England. The war was going badly for France in 1429 until Joan stepped in and, for the first time, solidly united the French-speaking people behind their monarch. She had an enormous impact on the course of history, but when it became expedient to get her out of the way, Church and state worked perfectly together to achieve the end.

Joan of Arc was tried for witchcraft and heresy in 1431 and found guilty. The witchcraft charge was based on her seemingly supernatural powers in battle, and her visions of angels and saints and hearing them speak. It must be remembered that at this period of history it was common for religious persons to see visions of the Savior, the Virgin, and saints. Joan's visions, however, were adjudged to be superstitious and proceeding from evil and diabolical spirits.

Among the heresy charges were Joan's short hair and the wearing of men's clothes while taking the sacrament; believing in saints and angels as firmly as in Christ; predicting the future; believing in her visions without consulting any churchman, and rejecting the judgment of the Church as God on earth.

Under pressure, Joan confessed to all of the crimes and was received back into the Church. But later, she retracted her confession and went back to wearing men's clothing and reaffirmed that she did hear voices of saints. The Church then decided that she was a heretic after all and turned her over to the state to be executed.

Joan of Arc was burned at the stake in Rouen, France on May 30, 1431. The Church court reopened her case in 1455 and though long dead, Joan was declared innocent. Almost five hundred years later, the ex-witch became a saint. She was beatified in 1909 and canonized by Pope Benedict XV in 1920. What *was* Joan of Arc, witch or saint? Clearly, there was much confusion over her case throughout a long period of years.

There is confusion to this day. True, Joan was a great heroine and a girl of courage and valor. She bravely led the men of Orleans to victory against the English and had Charles VII crowned King of France. Soon afterward, however, the king lost interest in Joan and her "voices from God" and ceased to protect her.

At her trial, Joan absolutely refused to say the

As can be seen in this 1854 portrait by Ingres, five centuries after her death, Joan of Arc was considered a saint rather than a witch.   THE GRANGER COLLECTION.

Lord's Prayer. This was a significant piece of evidence against her because it was widely believed that witches were unable to utter the prayer. Also, she had danced around the fairy tree at Domrémy, a well-known witches' activity. When asked to describe the voices that guided her, she said that she could "see them walking around amongst the Christians."

Joan also spoke of visits from a Saint Michael. Since the inquisitors hoped to prove that this Saint Michael was really an incubus (demon), they asked Joan if he appeared clothed or naked. She refused to answer the question. Whatever her reasons, Joan did not make things easy for herself.

After she was burned, her ashes were thrown into the river. Some historians said that this was done so that her remains could not be used as relics by those who believed in her sainthood. And then there were those who said that Joan's ashes were thrown into the water at the exact spot where human sacrifices had been made in ancient times.

Another trial that achieved great notoriety was that of Lady Alice Kyteler in Kilkenny, Ireland, in 1324. It is of particular interest because it demonstrates the clearcut difference in treatment of rich and poor by the courts.

Lady Alice was married to her fourth husband,

and she had a son, William Outlawe, born of her first marriage. The mother was said to have brought her son great wealth by using magic. Every morning she swept the streets of Kilkenny (shocking for a lady of her station!) in the direction of William's door while chanting:

> To the house of William my son
> Hie all the wealth of Kilkenny town!

Observing this strange behavior, Lady Alice's husband suddenly became a bit anxious about what had happened to husbands one, two, and three. It occurred to him that they might have been bewitched —and if they had, he might be next. Since no one doubted the power of bewitchment, the gentleman made a formal complaint and Lady Alice was brought to trial before the Bishop of Ossory.

Torture was illegal throughout England, and no one was so foolhardy as to break the law while dealing with the wealthy and important Lady Alice. She kept her silence, and the trial came to a standstill. But the lady's servant, Petronilla de Meath, was another matter. Petronilla was flogged six times during the course of her questioning, and in no time at all she was willing to admit anything the court wanted to know. She confessed that she and her mistress were both witches. She said they had sacrificed cocks at the crossroads. They went to meetings at night. They lighted candles and cursed their enemies from the tops of their heads to the soles of their feet. They made magic potions from the entrails of cocks, hair, fingernails of corpses, and brains of unbaptized babies. Such messes were boiled in the skull of a hanged robber. In addition to these crimes, her servant said that Lady Alice had a familiar who appeared in the form of a cat or a dog. Petronilla also accused Lady Alice of having a lover—none other than the Grand Master whom she called Robin Artisson.

When Lady Alice's house was searched, two damning pieces of evidence were found: a flying stick, all smeared with ointment, and a Holy Wafer with the Devil's name stamped on it.

Alice Kyteler had money and important friends. She left for England at once, and we know no more about her. Nor do we know whether she was a witch or a slightly eccentric lady who liked to sweep the street and who had bad luck in husbands!

We *do* know what happened to Petronilla. She was publicly burned to the apparent delight of a very large audience.

Mother Samuel (also spelled Samwell) was a poor old lady who lived in Warboys, England. It was her simple pleasure to visit her well-to-do neighbors, the Throgmortons. These good people had five daughters and quite a few servants as well. It must have been a bustling household, but suddenly, one day in 1589, everyone fell completely silent and stared at ten-year-old Jane. She was rolling on the floor, seized with violent convulsions. She recovered in a few minutes, but from that time on, she had the same kind of fit at least once every day.

No one knew what to do, and Jane continued to have fits—and lots of attention. On one occasion, right in the middle of a seizure, she pointed her finger at Mother Samuel and hollered, "Witch!"

In a society where everyone lived in deadly fear of witches, this was, of course, a highly sensational accusation. The other Throgmorton children sensed its dramatic possibilities immediately, and from then on, all five of them had fits regularly. They all said that Mother Samuel had bewitched them. The parents, strangely, seemed only half convinced. They asked Mother Samuel to remove the spell but continued to welcome her in their house.

The old woman insisted that she didn't have anything to do with the fits and the elder Throgmortons must have believed her because the situation remained unchanged and went on for months.

Then one day in 1590, a Lady Cromwell visited the afflicted household. She was shocked by what she saw and promptly decided that if the parents were too stupid, or too lazy to do anything to help their poor children, she would take matters into her own hands. She grabbed hold of Mother Samuel and seizing a knife, hacked off a lock of the old lady's hair. She then gave it to Mrs. Throgmorton and told her that if she would burn it in the fire the spell would be broken. (We don't know whether Mrs. Throgmorton followed the directions or not.)

Mother Samuel, usually calm and pleasant, was naturally upset about the indignity of such rough handling, and she mumbled something under her breath. No one heard what she said, but that mumble was to be remembered for a long time.

The very same night, Lady Cromwell dreamed that she was attacked by a cat. Her daughter-in-law, who slept in the same room, heard her struggling and fighting in her sleep. The next day, her Ladyship became very ill. She remained so for two years and finally died in 1592.

During all of this time, the Throgmorton children were still having fits, and the parents, still undecided, from time to time asked Mother Samuel to remove her spell. Finally, apparently worn out (or bored) by the whole matter, she said that yes, she *was* a witch but had broken the spell. Now everyone rejoiced, the children recovered, and all was well for a time. But then the old lady must have realized that she had been foolish and could get into really serious trouble, so she withdrew her confession and said that the recovery of the children had been a coincidence.

But at once, with renewed vigor and energy, the Throgmorton girls fell into terrifying fits again. If the parents had had doubts about Mother Samuel's guilt, they had them no longer. They had the woman arrested and taken before the magistrate. In a tiny village court, she was accused not only of bewitching the children but of murdering Lady Cromwell with a mumbled curse. In addition, Mother Samuel's husband and daughter were charged with being her accomplices. All three were hanged at Huntingdon in 1593.

Upon the death of the Samuel family, their very modest household goods went to Sir Henry Cromwell who happened to be Lord of the Manor. Although this was accepted procedure Sir Henry had no personal use for the paltry sum the estate brought at sale. He used it to arrange for an annual sermon against witchcraft. With the addition of some further contributions, the sermon was preached every single year until well into the eighteenth century!

The case of Mother Samuel, or the Case of the
Warboy Witches as it is more commonly known, is
one of many in which hysterical children were responsible for the deaths of accused witches.

In England witches were usually hanged rather than
burned. This is a woodcut of the Chelmsford witch
trial of 1589.        THE GRANGER COLLECTION.

Another case that, with a few variations, turns up again and again, is that of convent witches. Today, with our sophisticated knowledge of psychology, we know that a young girl, shut away in a convent and totally deprived of the company of the opposite sex, may engage in all sorts of fantasies. Either through guilt feelings or wish fulfillment, she may come to believe that the fantasies are real. But in the Middle Ages, fantasy was often confused with fact and the result could be dramatic. A typical example is this story of French witch-nuns.

In 1607, a very small Ursuline convent in Aix-en-Provence, France, opened its doors to a four-teen-year-old novice named Madeleine de la Palud. Madeleine was a model novice for two years, then suddenly she began to have fits. She shook from head to foot and insisted that she was surrounded by devils. In no time at all, some of the other nuns began to have the same symptoms.

The director of the convent, Father Romillon, was mystified by this turn of events and believed that Madeleine was possessed by a devil. He decided to perform a ceremony to exorcise the devil and fully expected that life in the convent would return to normal. He couldn't have been more wrong. Not only did Father Romillon fail to exorcise the imp, but Madeleine went from bad to worse and told an incredible story (which, in

part, might have been true). She said that a year
before she had entered the convent, she had been
seduced by her village priest, one Father Gauffridi. They carried on a love affair for some time,
and Father Gauffridi told Madeleine that although he was unable to marry her before God, he
would do so before the Devil. They married at a
Devil's Mass and, in the process, Madeleine had
become a witch.

Poor Father Romillon, with this tale and six
"possessed" nuns on his hands, was beside himself.
Somewhat strangely, considering the climate of the
time, the priest never seemed to consider the possibility that Madeleine really *was* a witch, even
though she insisted that it was so. He simply took
Madeleine and another nun, Louise Capeau, to a
Father Michaelis to see if he might have better
luck at exorcising the nuns' devils. He had not—
and this time, *both* girls told stories of intimacies
with Father Gauffridi. Father Michaelis ordered
an inquisition—but for the priest, not the girls who
were presumably his victims.

Gauffridi was tried, was found to have Devil's
Marks and perished at the stake. Madeleine made
an immediate recovery and lived to be seventy
years of age. Unfortunately, we have no records of
what happened to the other witches of Aix-en-
Provence.

# 6

# Some Famous Warlocks

The word "warlock," no longer in style, is sometimes used to mean a male witch.

The male witch has always been a comparative rarity. True, there were some men like Mr. Samuel or Father Gauffridi who were condemned as witches, but it is doubtful that they were guilty. While a good many men dabbled in occult matters, they were much more apt to be magicians, alchemists, or sorcerers. Sometimes, the distinctions between such practitioners were very unclear.

The position of the Church on the occult arts throughout the Middle Ages adds to the confusion because of its lack of consistency. At times, occult

From our own point of view, it could be stated that witchcraft was a religion while other forms of supernatural practice were nothing of the sort.

Unlike witches, who were in the main rather ignorant, alchemists and magicians were often among the most intelligent and well-informed men of their day. Some were intellectuals, the forerunners of the scientific age that was to follow; many were charlatans who made a brilliant success of cheating the public.

It is interesting to note that even when the inquisition was persecuting sorcerers, princes and clerics alike consulted them on occasion or sought their services surreptitiously.

One wonders if the Devil or Grand Master of the coven often was an opportunist, or if he was really a believer, a true warlock. While these men were frequently known in the community, they were almost never arrested. It seems that they were considered so powerful no one dared to risk their wrath. It was safer to leave them alone.

Since there was so little trial testimony, almost nothing was recorded. But scarce as warlock stories are, we do have a few. A very early one dates from England in 1324. Robert le Mareschal of Leicester was a roomer at the house of John de Nottingham, better known as the Witch of Coventry. One day,

In the Middle Ages almost any poor, elderly, eccentric person—man or woman—ran the risk of being accused of witchcraft.

activities were considered permissible if they did not involve heresy. But at other times, it was decreed that it was impossible to foretell the future, locate stolen articles, practice medicine with the help of astrology, or to make philters (potions) without invoking the help of demons.

While the dictionary is of little help in distinguishing between sorcery and witchcraft, a loose definition during the Middle Ages may have been that the witch had presumably made a pact with the Devil and had forsaken Christianity. This was not necessarily true of the other occult practitioners.

twenty-seven good men of the town visited the famous witch and offered him a large sum of money to murder the king, the prior of Coventry, and several other people. A deal was quickly made and with le Mareschal as his helper, the witch got to work.

The first thing the two men did was to make waxen images of the six men they planned to kill. Being careful workmen, however, they decided to try out the method on someone unimportant first. They selected a townsman named Richard de Sowe and made a seventh doll in his image. Then they drove a lead nail through its forehead.

Unwilling to leave anything to chance, they wandered over to de Sowe's house to see what was happening. The man was screaming with a headache and seemed to be totally out of his mind.

De Nottingham and le Mareschal rushed home, pulled the nail out of the doll's forehead, and stuck it into the heart instead. Three days later, de Sowe was dead.

Either le Mareschal was terrified by this success —or else he had a falling out with his teacher. In any case, he reported the entire story to the authorities. He was given his freedom in exchange for the information. John de Nottingham was arrested and died in prison while awaiting trial.

Another warlock, Major Thomas Weir of Edinburgh was known to be a most pious Presbyterian gentleman. (In fact, he was *so* pious that we are somehow reminded of the convent witches and their frustration fantasies!) Imagine the shocked excitement among his neighbors when Major Weir suddenly announced that he had been a witch all his life. He also involved his sister, Jane, and they were both tried in 1670.

It is hard to say which of the two was more outspoken—or perhaps more insane. The major seemed to enjoy telling in detail about the indecent relationships he had carried on for years with his sister, his stepdaughter, and the housemaid. Fantasy or fact? No one will ever know. The major also boasted about his extraordinary supernatural powers and said that they all came from the carved wooden staff that he always carried.

Sister Jane corroborated all the stories. In addition, to prove her own supernatural power, she told about the "fairy" who came at her bidding to help her spin yarn. Jane also described the Devil's Mark on her brother's shoulder.

Jane was hanged. Thomas was strangled and then burned. When he was thrown into the flames, his Devil's staff was thrown in with him.

Dr. John Fian was one of a group of witches

tried at North Berwick, Scotland, in 1591. King James VI was particularly interested in this case because he had reason to believe that a number of these witches were plotting against his life.

Under torture, Fian confessed that he was the secretary of the witches. He had a list of all their names, and it was his job to prepare the written Pacts with the Devil.

Plots on the king's life were fashionable among sixteenth-century English witches. This 1591 woodcut shows witch Agnes Sampson and her coven raising a storm against the king's ship.  THE  GRANGER COLLECTION.

Later, Fian retracted his confession and a publication of the day had a report of the events that followed. This article appeared in *Newes from Scotland* in 1591, and it gives us a good idea not only of the cruelty that was inflicted at the witch trials, but of the matter-of-fact way in which it was reported:

His nails upon all his fingers were riven and pulled off with an instrument called in Scottish a Turkas, which in English we call a pair of pincers, and under every nail there was thrust two needles over even up to their heads. At all of which torments notwithstanding the Doctor never shronke any whit, neither would he then confess it the sooner for all the tortures inflicted upon him.

Then was he with all convenient speed, by commandment, conveyed again to the torment of the boots, wherein . . . his legs were crushed and beaten . . . whereby they were made unserviceable for ever. And notwithstanding all these grievous pains and cruel torments he would not confess anything, so deeply had the devil entered his heart that he utterly denied all that which he had before avouched, and would say nothing thereunto but this, that what he had done and said before was only done and said for fear of pains which he had endured.

. . . the said Doctor Fian was soon arraigned, condemned and adjudged by the law to die, and then to be burned according to the law of the land, provided in that behalf. Whereupon he was put into a cart, and being first strangled, he was immediately put into a great fire, being ready provided for that purpose, and there burned in the Castle hill of Edinburgh on a Saturday in the end of January last past, 1591.

# 7

# The Witches of Salem

The witchcraft of Europe came to America when the Europeans came. The American Indians, like primitive peoples everywhere, had many beliefs and practices that were common to pagan religions, but the colonists had little interest in—or knowledge of—Indian religious rites. White people, however, were observed by their neighbors, and then as now, unusual behavior was usually found suspicious.

Settlers were arriving in the New World during the most frenzied period of the witch hunts in Britain and Europe. Perhaps it was inevitable that they brought their European attitudes with them.

New England lost little time in putting anti-witch laws on its books. A Massachusetts law of 1641 said: "Witchcraft which is fellowship by covenant with a familiar spirit to be punished with death." The similar law of Connecticut, written a year later stated: "If a man or woman be a witch, that is, hath or consulteth with a familiar spirit, they shall be put to death." There were a few scattered witch killings here and there over a period of years. Then suddenly, in the year 1692 . . .

Salem, in the Massachusetts Bay Colony, was a quiet little town. Most of the residents were faithful churchgoers and their Congregationalist minister was the Reverend Samuel Parris.

The minister lived with his wife, his nine-year-old daughter Elizabeth, an eleven-year-old niece, Abigail Williams, and a West Indian servant, Tituba. The children listened eagerly to the exciting tales of witchcraft that Tituba had brought from her native island. West Indies witchcraft had its roots in African practices, and Tituba's stories must have fascinated the girls. On the other hand, Tituba must have been just as excited by the kind of witch gossip the children heard from their elders. The stories all blended together and stimulated everyone's imagination.

One day, after a particularly vivid conversation

about witches, the girls began to act very oddly. They said things that made no sense, rolled on the floor, and stood in strange postures. For Puritan girls who had been brought up very strictly, this was extremely peculiar behavior. And especially in the home of the minister! The neighbors came to see, and it didn't take them long to decide that the girls were having fits.

Reverend Parris knew all about fits. It was clear that the girls were possessed or bewitched, and he insisted that they name their tormentor. They named Tituba.

When questioned, Tituba confessed that she was a member of a coven, that she had signed the Devil's book, and that the Devil had ordered her to afflict the girls. There were rumors at the time that Tituba's confession was "encouraged" by several beatings from the Reverend Parris. (Later, Tituba would admit that she *had* been beaten, but by then, it was all quite complex.)

Possibly in an effort to draw attention away from herself at the outset, Tituba named one Sarah Good as a witch and suggested that a few other local residents were witches as well.

By this time, the two bewitched girls were the center of attraction in the village. But they could not long hold the center of the stage without competition. They were soon joined in their antics by nine or ten other girls. The entire group behaved particularly disgracefully in church, yelling, falling down, rolling in the aisle, and interrupting prayers.

Clearly this could not be allowed to continue, and, in an effort to put an end to it, all of those whom the girls or Tituba had named as witches were immediately called to trial. Following the outrageous practice of European trials, one of the witnesses was Sarah Good's four-year-old daughter, Dorothy. The child testified, in answer to questions, that her mother kept a yellow bird (a familiar), and the four-year-old's statements were unhesitatingly entered into the court records.

Shortly after Dorothy's appearance in court, the bewitched girls showed marks on their arms that they said came from Dorothy's teeth. Not in spite of, but *because* Dorothy had never been close enough to the girls to bite them, the little child was arrested and put on trial with the other accused witches. It was assumed that she could inflict teeth marks across a room. This kind of evidence of supernatural power was called *spectral* evidence and was always welcomed at a witch trial.

During the trial, Sarah Good stoutly denied that she was a witch—but every time she looked in the

A nineteenth-century illustration of Sarah Good's trial
showing the young girls giving *spectral* evidence.

direction of the "afflicted" children, they all fell to the floor in fits. They said they could see her yellow bird flying around her head and a black man whispering in her ear. The fact that no one else could see these things did not trouble the judges. It was more spectral evidence and was completely acceptable to the court.

Finally, Sarah Good declared that it was not she, but Mother Osborne, a woman who had long been bedridden, who had bewitched the girls. Mother Osborne was accused. Abigail Williams, another townswoman, came forward and announced that she had had a vision of a sabbat in which she recognized several members of the church congregation taking part in a Black Mass. They were all accused. So was a Congregationalist minister.

The list grew longer, and hysteria swelled like a tropical storm. Everyone was caught up in it, and no one was safe. A child's "vision" or testimony about "torments," the finding of a Witch's or Devil's Mark, a coincidence of illness, death, or misfortune following a neighbor's visit—any one of these things was enough to bring an arrest. The madness spread from Salem to other towns.

But just as swiftly as the storm had come, it passed. The entire Salem witch hunt had lasted from March to September, 1692. During that time, more than one hundred fifty persons had been arrested, twenty-one had lost their lives.

The witch hunt may have died so rapidly because attitudes were changing and by 1692, the worst period of persecution on the Continent was over. Or perhaps, on a more personal level, in a tiny village the size of Salem, when 150 arrests had been made, the madness of it all began to be obvious.

When the hysteria dissolved it dissolved so completely that in 1697, one of the afflicted girls, the entire jury, and the presiding judge, Samuel Sewall, all confessed publicly that they had made a mistake and begged for forgiveness.

By 1711, the entire affair seemed so ludicrous that the Massachusetts General Court reversed the decision against most of the "witches" and paid back their survivors for the costs of the trials. It was one of the very odd features of the law at that time that all accused persons had to pay room and board while they were in jail—even if they were ultimately found to be innocent. If they were hanged, their families had to pay the hangman's fee!

In spite of the general feelings of remorse and shame, there were still a few die-hards. Foremost among these were Increase Mather, president of Harvard, and his son Cotton, both authors of works about witchcraft. Cotton Mather's most famous book was called *The Wonders of the Invisible World*. It was published while the trials were in progress and helped to stimulate fear at the time. Mather continued to write in the same vein until 1728, but by then he had lost almost all of his followers.

The end of the Salem story is that in 1957, the Commonwealth of Massachusetts freed from blame every one of the "witches." It was a just act—but of little help to those who had lost their lives, or even their reputations, their health, or their property. And it took 265 years!

CONDEMNED AT THE SALEM TRIALS

| | |
|---|---|
| Bishop, Bridget | Hanged, June 10. |
| Bradbury, Mary | Convicted, September 6. Escaped. |
| Burroughs, Rev. George | Hanged, August 19. |
| Carrier, Martha | Hanged, August 19. |
| Cloyce, Sarah | Convicted, September 6. Reprieved. |
| Cory, Giles | Pressed to death, September 19. |
| Eames, Rebecca | Convicted, September 17. Reprieved. |
| Esty, Mary | Hanged, September 22. |
| Faulkner, Abigail | Convicted. Spared because pregnant. |

As in the case of Joan of Arc, the Salem witchcraft executions looked different to later generations. This 1869 painting by Thomas Satter Noble is entitled "The Salem Martyr." WIDE WORLD PHOTOS.

| | |
|---|---|
| Foster, Ann | Died in prison. |
| Good, Sarah | Hanged, July 19. |
| Hoar, Dorcas | Convicted, September 6. Reprieved. |
| Hobbs, Abigail | Convicted, September 6. Reprieved. |
| How, Elizabeth | Hanged, July 19. |
| Jacobs, George | Hanged, August 19. |
| Lacy, Mary | Convicted, September 6. Reprieved. |
| Martin, Susanna | Hanged, July 19. |
| Nurse, Rebecca | Hanged, July 19. |
| Osborne, Sarah | Died in prison. |
| Parker, Alice | Hanged, September 22. |
| Parker, Mary | Hanged, September 22. |
| Proctor, Elizabeth | Convicted. Spared because pregnant. |
| Proctor, John | Hanged, August 19. |
| Pudeator, Ann | Hanged, September 22. |
| Reed, Wilmot | Hanged, September 22. |
| Scott, Margaret | Hanged, September 22. |
| Tituba | Imprisoned. |
| Wardwell, Samuel | Hanged, September 22. |
| Wilds, Sarah | Hanged, July 19. |
| Willard, John | Hanged, August 19. |

# 8

## White Witchcraft, or *Beneficia*

The white witch has turned up wherever there has been witchcraft. She practices only white magic, or *beneficia* (beneficial magic). The white witch is said to have the power to cure illness, remove a wart, make a potion or a spell for good purposes such as attracting a desired lover, finding a lost object, or bringing about a hoped-for pregnancy. Most important, the white witch is supposed to protect against black magic, *maleficia*.

The white witch was often the doctor of the community—and still is today in certain areas. Possibly no one else has ever been as highly skilled in the use of herbal remedies.

During the days of the witch hunts, the white witch was just as cruelly hunted and punished as the black witch. Even though she may have done none but good deeds, it was assumed that she could only have gotten the special power to do them from the Devil. Many an old woman, wise in the ways of healing, cured a sick neighbor and was killed for her trouble.

Long before medical science developed, some people were well versed in the use of herbs and could concoct very effective remedies with them.

In addition to herbs, the white witch resorted to charms. They sound particularly unimpressive today. The Old English rhyme that follows was a charm against evil spirits.

> Black-luggie, hammer-head,
> Rowan-tree, and red thread
> Put the warlocks to their speed.

The rowan tree was known to be a particularly potent protection against witches.

$$
\begin{array}{ccccc}
S & A & T & O & R \\
A & R & E & P & O \\
T & E & N & E & T \\
O & P & E & R & A \\
R & O & T & A & S \\
\end{array}
$$

This magic square is a very, very old one and has been used for countless purposes. It was even believed to cure sick animals. The "directions for use" were to draw the square on a piece of paper, tear it up, and mix it with the animal's food.

Here is another ancient all-purpose charm:

Carry the right eye of a wolf inside your right sleeve and you will be safe from all injuries.

Johann Weyer, in 1568, advised reciting the following to cure a toothache:

Galbes, galbat, galdes, galdat.

This same white witch had a cure for hydrophobia, too. The patient was instructed to eat a piece of apple on which was written:

Hax, pax, max
Deus adimax.

In England, the following charm was used to protect one against marsh-fever:

Nail three horseshoes to the bedpost and say:

Father, Son and Holy Ghost
Nail the Devil to this post.
Thrice I smite with Holy Crok
With this mell I thrice do knock,
One for God,
And one for Wod,
And one for Lok.

The Christian elements in the above charm are quite clear. Wod and Lok refer to Wodan and Loki, two ancient Norse gods. It is a good example of the mixture of Christianity and paganism that appears over and over again.

Some of the charms and spells sound *purely* Christian in content—but they were used for witchcraft. In 1527, William Browne claimed to have cured a sick horse by using certain herbs and then reciting the Lord's Prayer, five Hail Marys, and three Apostles' Creeds.

A few years later, Agnes Robson told her bishop that she cured pigs by saying:

God almighty, good and holy charity, I beseech you of your blessed goodness to help this thing.

> John is thy christen name, John
> And three bitter hath thee bitten,
> Three bitter bitter hath thee nippen,
> And three bitter bitter hath thee stricken.

Beseeching Almighty God, whether it were eye or tongue or heart, the better shall be your heal and boot, the Father, the Son and the Holy Ghost.

There is a striking similarity in a charm that was cited in the confession of Anna Whittle, a convicted witch of Lancaster, England:

> Three Biters hast thou bitten,
> The heart, ill Eye, ill Tongue;

Three bitter shall be thy Boot,
Father, Son, and Holy Ghost
   a God's name.
Five Pater-nosters, five Aves, and a Creed,
In worship of five wounds of our Lord.

White witches did not always use charms like
these. They had other means of protection, and some
of them are far from appealing. If you ever feel
that you are in danger of being bewitched, you
might:

- Carry the tooth of a corpse.
- Stand in the smoke of a burning corpse.
- Smear yourself with the gall of a crow.

As already mentioned, throughout the period of
the witch hunts, anyone who consulted a witch was
just as liable to punishment as the witch. One such
client was apprehended and during her confession
at the trial she explained how the witch had cured
her arthritis. She had been told to:

... take hog's dung and charnel and put them
together and hold them in her left hand, and to
take in the other hand a knife, and to prick the
medicine three times, and then to cast the same
into the fire, and to take the said knife, and to
make three pricks under a table, and to let the
knife stick there. And after that to take three

leaves of sage, and as much of her John (herb grace) and put them into ale, and drink it last at night and first in the morning; and that she taking the same, had ease of her lameness.

It was generally believed that any person could break a spell, if he knew the witch who had cast it. One way was to find the witch and scratch her skin until blood appeared. Then, the bewitched person cut his nails and threw them into a fire; immediately afterward, he washed his hands in a basin of water and threw the water into the fire.

In addition to other services, the white witch also made amulets, small objects carried or worn on the body for protection against bewitchment. They often contained the entrails of animals or humans plus an assortment of herbs. Amulets are still used in some places today. And "descendants" of amulets are common all over the civilized world. Have you ever worn a charm bracelet or a religious medal?

Another remnant of the old superstitions is our use of mistletoe at Christmas time. Once mistletoe was considered to be a precious charm. Since it grows on trees and not on the ground, it was believed that witches were totally powerless near it.

Back in the Middle Ages, the same kind of peo-

A diagram for the construction of a seventeenth-century magic circle used for the purpose of gaining wealth, not for evil power.

ple who now write letters to the Lonelyhearts column of the newspaper went to the white witch instead. She had many recipes for attracting and capturing the love object. A very popular one was to make a heart out of wax. The heart was then melted in a fire while the witch muttered appropriate magic incantations over it. As the wax melted, it caused the real-life beloved to "melt with love."

# 9

## A Compendium of *Maleficia*

The black witch had a terrifying collection of charms, spells, incantations, and brews, but it is probable that the real secrets of those for whom witchcraft was a religion were never divulged. If that is the case, then we really know nothing of the religious practices of witches. Much of the information that we do have, aside from confessions of people who were either deluded or under torture and from old books of magic of doubtful authorship, comes from a particularly evil and curious document full of unfounded "facts." This was known as *The Malleus Maleficarum,* or The Witch's Hammer.

The volume was written by two Dominican monks, Jacob Sprenger and Heinrich Kramer, in either 1486 or 1490. It went into dozens of editions in at least four languages and became known as the witch-hunter's Bible. It gave careful instructions for hunting and finding witches as well as the best methods for conducting trials that would lead to conviction. The book was so popular in so many countries that much of the information in it has been handed down as authentic although most of it was sheer invention.

Another source of information was the group of medieval magic books known as *grimoires*. Although a great deal of this material can still be found in rare book collections today, there is no reason to believe that it had anything to do with The Old Religion.

From such books on the arts of *maleficia*, we learn that a witch could supposedly cause a storm by killing a black cat at a crossroads.

A witch was also presumed to be capable of performing *sympathetic magic*. By this means, a victim could be injured from a distance by using a doll or an image to represent him. In addition to being stuck with pins or nails, the dolls could be melted in a fire. As they melted away, life flowed from a victim.

Then there was the "evil eye." It was thought that the witch could cast a spell with a stare or even a brief glance. Many persons were convicted as witches because they had a squint or were cross-eyed.

Among "recipes" of witchcraft, we find two for:

### FLYING OINTMENT

1. Black dust of tomb, venom of toad, flesh of

In this illustration for a late seventeenth-century book by Cotton Mather, witches consult with the Devil about performing sympathetic magic.

brigand, lung of ass, blood of blind infant, corpses from graves and bile of ox.

2. Infant's fat, juice of cowbane, aconite, cinquefoil, deadly nightshade, soot.

And here are a pair of recipes for:

### KILLING OINTMENT

1. Hemlock, water of aconite, poplar leaves, soot.

2. Water hemlock, sweet flag, cinquefoil, bat's blood, belladonna, oil.

Margaret Murray points out that if witches in truth used these formulae, they were undoubtedly as sophisticated as reputed in their knowledge of herbs. Aconite, belladonna, and hemlock were the most poisonous plants growing freely in Europe.

*The Malleus Maleficarum* gives us the following information on invoking the Devil:

Satan may be invoked under a variety of names, each having a special etymological significance. As Asmodeus, he is the Creature of Judgement. As Satan, he becomes the Adversary. As Behemoth, he is the Beast. Diabolus, the Devil, signifies Two Morsels: The Body and the soul, both of which he kills. Demon connotes Cunning over Blood. Belial, Without a Master, Beelzebub, Lord of Flies.

Even in the seventeenth century the Devil was thought
to appear with great flourish, in a cloud of smoke.

One of the grimoires tells exactly how to summon a demon. Repeat twice:

I conjure you, O spirit, to appear within a minute by the power of Great Adonai, by Eloim, by Ariel, Johavam, Agla, Tagla, Mathon, Oarios, Almouzin, Arios, Membrot, Varvis, Pithona, Magots, Silphane, Rabost, Salamandrae, Tabost, Gnomus, Terreae, Coelis, Godens, Aqua, Gingua, Janua, Etituamus.

Or another way:

Eheieh
Iod
Tetragrammaton Elohim
El
Elohim Gibor
Eloah Va-Daath
El Adonai Tzabaoth
Elohim Tzabaoth
Shaddai

When you no longer want the demon around, you send him away as follows:

I am pleased and contented with thee, Prince Lucifer, for the moment. Leave thou in peace now, and go in quiet and without trouble. Do not forget our pact, or I will blast thee with my Wand. Amen.

From the confession of Isobel Gowdie, a convicted Scottish witch of the seventeenth century, we learn the formula used for changing into a cat:

I shall toe intill ane catt,
With sorrow, and sych, and a blak shott;
And I sall goe in the Divellis nam,
Ay will I com hom againe.

To return to human form:

Catt, catt, God send thee a blak shott.
I am in a cattis liknes just now,
Bot I sal be in a womanis liknes ewin now.
Catt, catt, God send thee a blak shott.

During her lengthy confession, Isobel Gowdie
also described how the coven raised a storm by
hitting a stone with a wet rag and saying:

I knock this rag upon this stone
To raise the wind in the Devil's name:
It shall not lie, until I please again.

The literature abounds in oaths to Satan. This
one is fairly typical:

We Lucifer, and all beforementioned and following spirits, swear to you, almighty God through
Jesus Christ of Nazarus, the Crucified One, our
conqueror, that we will faithfully perform everything written in this book: Also never to do you
any harm, either to your body or your soul, and to
execute everything immediately and without re-
fusing.

When *Newes from Scotland* reported the Fian
case, the article described how Dr. Fian broke his
pact with Satan:

Satan appeared all in blacke, with a white wande in his hande, demanded of him if hee would continue his faithful service, according to his first oath and promise made to that effect, whome (as hee then said) he utterly renounced to his face, and said unto him in this manner, "Avoide, Satan, avoide—I utterly forsake thee."

And pacts with Satan, whether made or broken, bring us naturally to the Black Mass, which holds

Mysterious symbols, often of a religious nature, were considered essential to the practice of witchcraft.

such a prominent place in popular witchcraft lore. Appropriately, then, we conclude our collection of *maleficia* with two black prayers recited at the Mass:

Lamb, which the priests of Adonai have made a symbol of sterility raised to the rank of a virtue, I sacrifice you to Lucifer. May the peace of Satan always be with you.

Astaroth, Asmodeus, I beg you to accept the sacrifice of this child which we now offer to you, so that we may receive the things that we ask.

Before we leave the Middle Ages, it is well to say a word about the decline of witchcraft and the persecution of witches.

Witchcraft hit its peak during the sixteenth century. Then, with the Age of Enlightenment, many changes occurred. Learning began to take the place of ignorance and superstition; science started to replace sorcery.

The new humanist movement led to a revival of interest in classical (pre-Christian) studies and as a result, religious influence began to lose some of its force. At the same time, Christian educators became interested in broader learning and gave up much of their rigid dogmatism for a new flexibility and reasonableness.

Science and art flourished in the new era of discovery and creativity; it was almost inevitable then, that as the theories of enlightenment spread, so did religious tolerance. The entire atmosphere changed and the inquisition slowly ground to a halt.

Both political and religious leaders began to speak out for understanding and acceptance of nonconformist ideas. And, with the spread of education and communication, more and more of the practitioners of The Old Religion were swept along in the general tide of progress and gave up their old ways.

The end did not come all at once, however. England held its last witchcraft trial in 1712. A woman was convicted, but her life was spared. A final conviction and execution took place in Scotland in 1722. Spain's last witch trial was held in 1782 and Germany's in 1793.

# 10

# Witchcraft Today

If you think that witchcraft is a thing of the past, you are very much mistaken. It has flourished for a long time in many parts of the world as far from each other as Africa, the West Indies, Polynesia and Pennsylvania.

While witchcraft never really died, little was heard of it in most parts of western Europe and the United States for many years. However, during the 1960's, there was a great revival of interest in the cult, and witches began popping up everywhere. In the main, these were new witches, converts. Unlike primitive rites of ancient times, or the prevailing ignorance and superstition of the

By the nineteenth century people took witches less seriously, but ideas about their appearance and behavior have persisted down to the present day.     THE GRANGER COLLECTION.

Middle Ages, today's witchcraft seems to be practiced on a mental rather than spiritual level. The practitioners have done their homework and learned a bit about ancient rites—but today's versions of the rites are at best a pale imitation, at worst, a travesty.

The following excerpts are from an article by Judy Klemesrud that appeared in *The New York*

*Times* on October 31, 1969. It is interesting to parallel the behavior discussed with what is known of witchcraft in the past.

Tonight is that spooky eve called Hallowe'en and it is the one night of the year when most of America's witches—whether hereditary, initiated or self-proclaimed—will be up to their usual tricks. Take Sybil Leek, the plump, British-born seeress who is probably the most-publicized witch in the world. Now a resident of Melbourne Beach, Fla., she will stop whatever she is doing at 9 P.M. to "take a little trip out of town" to visit a witches' coven in a location that she did not care to reveal.

Mrs. Raymond Buckland, the slender raven-haired high priestess of the Long Island witches' coven, will lead her group in an ancient ritual that includes hopping on broomsticks in the basement of her Brentwood, L.I., home.

And Mrs. Florence S. (she preferred not to be further identified), a Brooklyn housewife who owns a black cat named Thirteen, will once again don a large white sheet and playfully scare the neighborhood children who come to her home for tricks or treats.

These three women claim, with varying degrees

of seriousness, that they are witches. They are a part of the big boom in mysticism in this country, in which Americans are turning not only to witchcraft, but to astrology, fortune telling, Satanism, the psychic phenomena and other occult practices in what appears to be a search for either a serious spiritual experience—or a few laughs.

### UNIVERSITY COURSES

In fact, the interest in witchcraft is so great that several high schools and colleges, including the Universities of Alabama and South Carolina, have offered courses in it. At New York University's School of Continuing Education, 125 students enrolled in a course called "Witchcraft, Magic and Sorcery," forcing a move to a more spacious lecture room.

The 45-year-old Miss Leek, who is also a writer, a lecturer, an astrologer, a medium and a mother, thinks the wide interest in witchcraft (she calls it the "Old Religion") was "inevitable."

"We are entering the age of Aquarius, and people are searching," she said the other day in her suite at the New York Hilton. "They are searching for a religion where they don't have to live a God-like life, a religion that acknowledges them as human beings.

"Witchcraft," she went on, "is a return to a nature religion. It teaches people their place in the

Miss Sybil Leek, a modern British witch who is also an author and lecturer.    WIDE WORLD PHOTOS.

universe and helps them to see religion much more clearly—as a real thing and not as a fantasy world."

Miss Leek said she thought that witchcraft had a special appeal for the young.

"They feel that orthodox religion has let them down," she said.

"There is love in witchcraft," she added, "but not on a sentimental basis. We don't just say, 'Love thy neighbor as thyself.' We do. The action is more than the word."

Although she lives in Florida and will be moving to Houston early next year, Miss Leek is a member of a Boston coven. She said she knew of 400 covens now in existence throughout the United States, compared with 280 five years ago. There are three in the New York metropolitan area, she said, two in the city and one on Long Island.

The reddish-haired Miss Leek is what is known as a hereditary witch. She traces her witch-filled ancestry back to 1134 A.D. ("A family failing—it has to do with glands and the nervous system," she said.) A widow, she has two sons, Stephen, 20, a sound engineer who is not a witch, and Julian, 18, a photographer for *The Miami Herald* who has almost completed his studies to become a full-fledged witch.

"Almost 1,000 people tell me each week they want to be witches," said Miss Leek, who was in New York to plug her new book, "The Sybil Leek Book of Fortune Telling."

ANSWER IS SECRET

"I ask them why, and hardly any of them have
the right answer," she said. "Some of them will
giggle and say, 'I want to have fun' or 'I want to
have power.' Those are not the right answers.
There is only one, and of course I'm not going to
tell what it is."

Tonight's ceremony in the Bucklands' basement
will go something like this: First the witches remove their clothes and bathe in salt water to purify
themselves. Then, still nude (or "skyclad," as they
call it), they descend to the basement and step inside a 9-foot circle that is drawn about them with
a 400-year-old sword by Mrs. Buckland, the high
priestess, who is known in the Craft as Lady
Rowen. A bewitching ambiance is provided by
music from a tape recorder and incense burned in
a brass censer.

Once inside the circle, the witches will sing,
chant, dance with broomsticks in commemoration
of an ancient fertility rite, drink tea and wine, and
listen to the high priestess read from the Book of
Shadows.

The ceremony ends after Lady Rowen, dressed
only in a silver crown, bracelet, necklace and green
leather garter belt, takes a horned helmet and
places it on the head of her husband, the high
priest, who is known as Robat. This signifies that
power has been transferred from the high priestess
who reigns during the six months of summer, to the

high priest who rules during the six months of winter.

The Bucklands, who are "white," or good, witches, were initiated into the Craft in 1962 by the late well-known witch, Dr. Gerald Gardner, on the Isle of Man off the coast of their native England. Like most witches, they believe in reincarnation, and in retribution in this life.

"We believe that whatever you do—good or evil—will return to you three-fold in this life," Mrs. Buckland said recently.

Mr. Buckland, 35, is a slight, bearded editor of manuals for an overseas airline. He has a Ph.D. in anthropology from King's College in London. His 33-year-old wife works as a private secretary on Long Island. They have two sons, a 12-year-old who is a witch, and a 10-year-old who isn't.

The family gets along well with their neighbors, and the couple is frequently called upon to perform their wart cure on afflicted friends. Mrs. Buckland also makes tea of special herbs for people who have eye trouble. "It works wonders," she said.

### "FIRST-CLASS WITCH"

Black-haired, blue-eyed Mrs. Florence S. of Brooklyn is a self-proclaimed "A-No. 1, first-class witch" whose husband thinks she may be just that —especially when they are out sailing on Long Island Sound.

"When the wind stops, I stand up and say,

'Carabouch, send me a wind!' " she said. " 'Tell the sweet sisters of the south and west to send me a breeze.' And then, in a few minutes, the wind usually comes."

Mrs. S., who is in her forties, said that it was "taboo" for her to talk about all of her experiences with witchcraft. But she did say she had blessed a young ice skater named Kevin who had then gone on to win all of the ice skating contests he had entered.

### DISTRIBUTES LUCKY STONES

She also hands out small, smooth black stones called "gagis" to friends and relatives for good luck. She recently gave one to an unmarried woman and said that if the woman gave the gagi to the man she wanted to marry, he would be unable to refuse her.

Mrs. S. lives in a Victorian town house that she believes is haunted by a female spirit who lives in an upstairs linen closet. "I have seen her and I have felt her," she said. "One day she helped prevent me from falling down the basement stairs."

The slender mother of three said she had once made the mistake of dabbling in black magic, but added that she would never do it again.

"I lost my power for a year," she groaned, as her black cat, Thirteen, brushed up against her leg.

Another item in *The New York Times* reported

that a West Virginia man had gone to court to seek $150,000 in a slander suit against ten of his former neighbors. They had called him "a male witch, warlock and devil's consort." The defendants apologized, and the case was dropped.

Perhaps the most widespread resurgence of witchcraft is among young people. Covens have formed on college campuses everywhere, and some universities are offering courses in witchcraft. But you don't have to be a college student to be a witch.

An NBC television program, *First Tuesday,* presented a show called "The Witches of Squaresville," which pointed out the popularity of witchcraft among high school students. In fact, the commentator stated that nearly every self-respecting high school these days has its own practicing witch. The program showed two high school girls demonstrating a spell which, among other things, involved sticking three rose thorns into a mole's heart, then wrapping the heart in cloth. The girls recited incantations from a book they had borrowed from the public library.

Some young people claim that they are turning to witchcraft because their family religion does not fulfill their needs or give them the answers they seek. Some admit that they find it exciting, stimulating, "scary," or just plain fun. Psychologists think that acting out "black" rituals may be an outlet for feelings of aggression or hostility.

We are of course reminded here of the converted witch of the Middle Ages who joined the coven to wreak punishment on her neighbors, to indulge in licentious behavior that was outlawed in most social circles, or to find acceptance in a peer group.

And if present-day witches run the gamut from "born" witches like Sybil Leek, to those who are looking for fun or an outlet for hostility—it sounds just like old times, doesn't it?

# Appendix

Excerpts from Some Documents Pertaining to Witchcraft in
Western Europe and in Salem, Massachusetts

## From the Ecclesiastical Canons of
## King Edgar, 959

We enjoin, that every priest zealously promote
Christianity, and totally extinguish every heathenism; and forbid will worshipings, and necroman-
cies, and divinations, and enchantments, and man
worshipings, and the vain practices which are carried on with various spells, and with "frithsploos,"
and with elders, and also with various other trees,
and with stones, and with many various delusions,

with which men do much of what they should not. And we enjoin, that every Christian man zealously accustom his children to Christianity, and teach them the Paternoster and the Creed. And we enjoin, that on feast days heathen songs and devil's games be abstained from.

## From the Laws of King Canute, 1017–1035

We earnestly forbid every heathenism: Heathenism is, that men worship idols; that is, that they worship heathen gods, and the sun or the moon, fire or rivers, water-wells or stones, or forest trees of any kind; or love witchcraft, or promote *morth-work* in any wise.

## The Cap. Episcopi, *attributed to the Council of Anquira, 9th Century*

Some wicked women, reverting to Satan, and seduced by the illusions and phantasms of demons, believe and profess that they ride at night with Diana on certain beasts, with an innumerable multitude of women, passing over immense distances, obeying her commands as their mistress, and evoked by her on certain nights. It were well if they alone perished in their infidelity and did not draw so many along with them. For innumerable multitudes, deceived by this false opinion, believe all this to be true, and thus relapse into pagan errors. Therefore, priests everywhere should preach that they know this to be false, and that such phantasms are sent by the Evil Spirit, who deludes them in dreams. . . . It is to be taught to all that he who believes such things has lost his faith, and he who has not the true faith is not of God, but of the devil.

### The Bull of Pope Innocent VIII, 1484

It has come to our ears that numbers of both sexes do not avoid to have intercourse with demons, Incubi and Succubi; and that by their sorceries, and by their incantations, charms, and conjurations, they suffocate, extinguish and cause to perish the births of women, the increase of animals, the corn of the ground, the grapes of the vineyard and the fruit of the trees, as well as men, women, flocks, herds, and other various kinds of animals, vines and apple trees, grass, corn and other fruits of the earth; making and procuring that men and women, flocks and herds and other animals shall suffer and be tormented both from within and without, so that men beget not, nor women conceive; and they impede the conjugal action of men and women.

## The apology offered by the jurors of the Salem trials, 1697

We whose names are underwritten, being in the year 1692 called to serve as jurors in court at Salem, on trial of many who were by some suspected guilty of doing acts of witchcraft upon the bodies of sundry persons.

We confess that we ourselves were not capable to understand nor able to withstand the mysterious delusions of the Powers of Darkness and Prince of the Air, but were, for want of knowledge in ourselves and better information from others, prevailed with to take up with such evidence against the accused as on further consideration and better information we justly fear was insufficient for the touching the lives of any (Deuteronomy 17.6) whereby we fear we have been instrumental with others, though ignorantly and unwittingly, to bring upon ourselves and this People of the Lord the guilt of innocent blood, which sin the Lord saith in scripture he would not pardon (2 Kings 24.4), that is, we suppose, in regard of his temporal judgments.

We do therefore hereby signify to all in general (and to the surviving sufferers in especial) our deep sense of sorrow for our errors in acting on such evidence to the condemning of any person, and do therefore humbly beg forgiveness, first of God for Christ's sake for this our error, and pray that God would not impute the guilt of it to ourselves nor others. And we also pray that we may be considered candidly and aright by the living sufferers as being then under the power of a strong and general delusion, utterly unacquainted with and not experienced in matters of that nature.

We do heartily ask forgiveness of you all, whom we have justly offended, and do declare according to our present minds, we would none of us do such things again on such grounds for the whole world, praying you to accept of this in way of satisfaction for our offense, and that you would bless the inheritance of the Lord, that He may be entreated for the Land.

| | |
|---|---|
| FOREMAN, *Thomas Fisk* | *Joseph Evelith* |
| *William Fisk* | *Thomas Perly, Sr.* |
| *John Batcheler* | *Thomas Perkins* |
| *Thomas Fisk, Jr.* | *Samuel Sayer* |
| *John Dane* | *Andrew Elliot* |

*Henry Herrick, Sr.*

### The confession of Anne Putnam, one of the afflicted girls of Salem, read from the pulpit of Salem Village Church in 1706

I desire to be humbled before God for that sad and humbling Providence that befell my father's family in the year about '92: that I, then being in my childhood, should by such a Providence of God be made an instrument for the accusing of several persons of a grievous crime, whereby their lives were taken away from them, whom now I have just grounds and good reason to believe they were innocent persons; and that it was a great delusion of Satan that deceived me in that sad time, whereby I justly fear I have been instrumental with others, though ignorantly and unwittingly, to bring upon myself and this land the guilt of innocent blood; though what was said or done by me against any person I can truly and uprightly say before God and man, I did it not out of any anger, malice, or ill-will to any person, for I had no such thing against any of them; but what I did was ignorantly, being deluded by Satan.

# A Brief Dictionary of Witchcraft

AMULET   An object that is worn as a protection against bewitchment.

AGRIPPA, CORNELIUS   Full name, Henry Cornelius Agrippa von Nettesheim, 1486–1535. Famous magician known throughout Europe. Considered by some to be a witch. Author of *The Occult Philosophy*.

ARCANA   The great secrets of nature that the alchemists tried to discover.

BENEFICIA   White witchcraft. Acts of goodness and helpfulness performed by a witch.

BLACK MAGIC   See MALEFICIA.

BLACK MASS   A witch ceremony that is a blasphemous mockery of the Catholic Mass.

BOOTS   A medieval torture device consisting of a vice that was fastened onto the legs and tightened until the bones were crushed. Often used during the witch hunts to obtain confessions.

CABALA (also KABBALA) Mystic Hebrew interpretation of the Scriptures dating from about the seventh century. Had a large influence on medieval occult science and thought.

CAGLIOSTRO, COUNT ALESSANDRO Also known as Guiseppe Balsamo, 1743–1795. Italian adventurer, alchemist, magician, and necromancer. Often considered to be a witch.

COVEN A group of witches usually consisting of a leader and twelve members.

CROWLEY, ALISTAIR A Scottish witch, 1875–1947. Founded a satanic cult with a temple in London and another in Italy. At his death, his followers performed a black magic ceremony at his funeral.

DEE, DR. JOHN Famous British mathematician and student of the secret arts, 1527–1608. Practiced astrology, crystalgazing and performed seances with the help of his associate, Edward Kelly. Often called a witch.

DEVIL'S MARK A mark given to a witch upon initiation into the coven: a tattoo, a bite mark, a paw print, etc.

DIVINATION Fortune telling. Foretelling the future by water, stars, dice, numbers, dreams, stones, or any other means.

ESBAT A meeting of one coven.

EVIL EYE The power to bewitch by a look or a glance. A look that causes some sort of misfortune to the one who receives it.

FAMILIAR A pet animal kept by a witch. It was a gift of the Devil (although it could be inherited) and was helpful in performing many sorts of magic. Its power lay in the fact that it was really an imp or a spirit in disguise.

FASCINATION Same as EVIL EYE.

GRIMOIRE A book that explained how feats of magic were performed. There were a number of grimoires published during the Middle Ages.

HAND OF GLORY A witch's "candle" used for casting a powerful spell. Prepared as follows: Wrap the hand of hanged man in a piece of shroud and squeeze out the blood. Pickle the hand in a crock with salt, saltpeter, and peppers. After two weeks, remove it and leave it in the sun until thoroughly dry. Burn the fingers like tapers.

HEX  A curse, or evil spell. Also, as a verb, to bewitch. Especially common in Pennsylvania Dutch area. From the German *hexe,* witch.

HOPKINS, MATTHEW  Famous witch hunter, trial judge, and torturer. Known as the Witch-finder General of England. Especially active 1645–1646 in which year he sent hundreds to the gallows.

INCUBUS  A male demon that has sexual intercourse with a woman.

INQUISITION  Inquiry of the Church into any deviation from its teachings. The inquisition against witches reached its peak with Pope Innocent VIII's Bull of 1484.

KABBALA  See CABALA.

KELLY, EDWARD  Astrologer and medium closely associated with Dr. Dee.

LADDER  A torture rack on which the victim's body was bound and stretched. Used during the witch trials.

LEFT-HAND PATH  Black magic, maleficia.

LYCANTHROPY  The practice of changing into the form of a wolf or other animal and traveling through the countryside at night to attack humans or animals.

MALEFICIA  Black magic. Acts of witchcraft that are evil or harmful.

MALLEUS MALEFICARUM  (The Witches' Hammer) A textbook of witch-hunting. Written in 1486 or 1490 by two Dominicans, Father Jacob (James) Sprenger and Father Heinrich (Henry) Kramer, chief inquisitors of Germany.

MANDRAKE (Also MANDRAGORE)    An herb with narcotic properties. The root resembles a human form. Much used in herbal concoctions.

METAMORPHOSIS    The change from human into animal form.

NECROMANCY    Divination.

POSSESSION    The state of being controlled by the Devil or a demon. The victim was not responsible for his demented behavior. Some common manifestations of possession were fits, convulsions, vomiting of pins and other strange objects, change of voice that was known as "belly speaking."

SABBAT    Meeting of all the witches of a district held on certain specific days of the year. A large festival to honor the Devil, featuring special ceremonies, dancing, feasting, orgies.

SUCCUBUS    A female demon that has sexual intercourse with men.

TRANSVECTION    A witch's flight through the air on a stick, a stool, or a familiar.

VENEFICIA    Poisoning

WALPURGIS NACHT (Walpurgis Night)    The night of April 30th, great spring festival of the pagans. A very important sabbat date. Called Roodmas in England.

WATER TEST or WATER ORDEAL    A frequently used test for witches. The accused was tied right thumb to left big toe, left thumb to right big toe, and thrown into water. If accused floated, guilt was assumed; if accused sank, innocence was assumed.

WEREWOLF    A human who appears in the form of a wolf.

WHITE WITCHCRAFT    See BENEFICIA.

WITCH FINDER    One who made a career of finding and persecuting witches.

WITCH'S MARK    Often used interchangeably with DEVIL'S MARK. More accurately, the extra teat with which a witch was supposed to suckle her imp or familiar.

# Bibliography

DARAUL, ARKON, *Witches and Sorcerers.* New York: Citadel Press, 1962. (paper)

FRAZER, SIR JAMES G., *The Golden Bough.* New York: Macmillan, 1951.

HANSEN, CHADWICK, *Witchcraft at Salem.* New York: NAL Signet, 1970. (paper)

HAYES, CARLTON J. H., *A Political and Cultural History of Modern Europe,* Vol. 1. New York: Macmillan, 1932.

HOLE, CHRISTINA, *Witchcraft in England.* New York: Collier Books, 1966. (paper)

HUGHES, PENNETHORNE, *Witchcraft.* Baltimore: Penguin Books, 1965. (paper)

HUXLEY, ALDOUS, *The Devils of Loudun.* New York: Harper and Row, 1959. (paper)

JACKSON, SHIRLEY, *Witchcraft of Salem Village.* New York: Random House, 1956.

LEA, HENRY CHARLES, *The Inquisition of the Middle Ages.*

Abridged by Margaret Nicholson. New York: Macmillan, 1961.

LEEK, SYBIL, *Diary of a Witch.* New York: NAL Signet, 1969. (paper)

LETHBRIDGE, T. C., *Witches.* New York: Citadel, 1968. (paper)

LEWIS, ARTHUR H., *Hex.* New York: Trident Press, 1969.

LUCAS, HENRY S., *The Renaissance and the Reformation.* New York and London: Harper, 1934.

MALINOWSKI, BRONISLAW, *Magic, Science and Religion and Other Essays.* Garden City: Doubleday Anchor, 1948. (paper)

————, *Sex, Culture and Myth.* New York: Harcourt, Brace and World, 1962.

MICHELET, JULES, *Joan of Arc.* Translated by Albert Guerard. Ann Arbor: University of Michigan, 1957.

MURRAY, MARGARET ALICE, *The Witch-Cult in Western Europe.* New York: Oxford University Press, 1962. (paper)

NEAL, JAMES A., *Jungle Magic.* New York: Paperback Library, 1969. (paper)

PARRINDER, GEOFFREY, *Witchcraft: European and African.* London: Faber and Faber, 1963. (paper)

QUENNELL, M., and C. H. B. QUENNELL, *Everyday Life in the New Stone, Bronze and Early Iron Ages.* New York: Putnam, 1923.

ROBBINS, ROSSELL HOPE, *The Encyclopedia of Witchcraft and Demonolgy.* New York: Crown, 1959.

SEABROOK, WILLIAM R., *Jungle Ways.* New York: Harcourt, Brace and World, 1931.

SETH, RONALD, *Witches and Their Craft.* New York: Award Books, 1969. (paper)

# Index

Page references for illustrations are in *italic* type.